The Call To Authenticity

How one man discovered
the essence of leadership

Steven L. Anderson, Ph.D.

Published by:

Dream Star Press, Inc.
4443 N. High St.
Columbus, Oh 43214
614-262-8725

ISBN number 0-9755015-0-X

Author: Steven L. Anderson
Title: The Call to Authenticity

Printed by:

Perfection Press, Inc.
1200 Industrial Dr.
Logan, Iowa 51546
1-800-334-2920

Dedication:

This book is dedicated to
Henry Leuchter, M.D.
Thank you for everything.
I will never forget what you have done for me.

Acknowledgments:

There are so many people who I want to thank for their help and support in writing this book. I would like to acknowledge the support I received from the following individuals.

*First and foremost, I want to thank my beloved wife, Charlisa. She is my greatest cheerleader and confidant. She supported me on this journey and she gave invaluable feedback as an editor. I could not dream of having a more wonderful partner and soulmate.

*My friend, Jim Anderson. He saw in me potential as a leadership consultant long before I realized I had the skill to do it. I thank him for his insight, support and feedback on this book.

*My brother, Chuck Anderson, who has been a great source of inspiration and support in my life. I also appreciate the assistance he gave me in writing this book.

*My friends and colleagues, Adam Minton, and Rishanna Denman, and my daughter, Molly who gave me invaluable feedback on this book.

*My children for being an endless source of amazement and satisfaction in my life.

*My parents for making me feel that I had something special to give.

*My siblings, friends and colleagues who have taught me so much about the fields of psychology, consulting and life, including Marie Evans, Ron Stiebler, Shannon Stacey, Tara Dzienny, Paul Anderson, Lu Stauffer, Helane Caniglia, Nick Anderson, Nancy Betz, Patti Hathaway, Paula Butterfield, Mark Henson, Mark Zucker, John Carpenter, John Miller, Mike McCartney, Charlie Dygert, Sandy Shulman, Julie Brodie, Don Levitt, Kevin Anderson, Bob Anderson, Dick Anderson, Mary Wood-Anderson, Sam Wenger, and David Wallace.

*All of the clients I have had the privilege to work with. It has been an honor to be allowed to become a part of your journey. The courage many of you have shown sometimes moves me to tears. Thank you for leading.

Invictus

Out of the night that covers me,
Black as the Pit from pole to pole,
I think whatever gods may be
For my unconquerable soul.

In the fell clutch of circumstance,
I have not winced or cried aloud;
Under the bludgeonings of chance
My head is bloody, but unbowed.

Beyond this place of wrath and tears
Looms but the horror of the shade.
And yet the menace of the years
Finds, and shall find me, unafraid.

It matters not how strait the gait,
How charged with punishments the scroll,
I am master of my fate:
I am captain of my soul.

William Ernest Henley (1849-1903)

Introduction

Why did I write this book? And what does authenticity have to do with leadership? Many people think leadership is a personality trait that some people have and others do not. I do not see it that way. In fact, the longer I live, the more I am convinced that leadership has nothing to do with who is following. I believe that leadership is an inner decision to be completely and authentically yourself all of the time. I believe that good leaders have a sense of what needs to be done at all times because they are guided by their inner sense of self, not by a need to control or gain approval from others. This concept is exciting to me because anyone can become a leader; all it takes is courage and a lot of hard work.

I wrote this book for one reason. I want to help you become the best leader you can become. I want to assist you in becoming the architect of your journey to authenticity, because I believe that journey is an important part of a good life.

I am writing this on a gorgeous autumn day in central Ohio. As I sit here on the patio of the lodge at Deer Creek State Park I am experiencing a feeling of complete inner peace. I look up at the azure blue skies and then my eyes wander through the tangled fingers of oak branches to the shimmering surface of the lake. It is a magnificent sight. As I am bathed in the warmth of the autumn sunshine, I feel lucky to be alive. As I embrace this scenery and allow it to permeate my soul, I am struck by how incredibly different this experience is from the intense pain and turmoil of my life just two decades ago.

At that time, in the most unlikely of places, when I least expected it, I was blessed with my first taste of the meaning of leadership. You see, at that time, I was severely mentally ill. I had struggled with depression and anxiety for about a decade. Toward the end, I wasn't sure if I wanted to live any more. I was waking up with panic attacks every night, and nearly passing out from anxiety during the day. My self-esteem was at rock bottom. I felt like a complete failure. I felt like I was trapped and I couldn't see any way out. I knew I couldn't withstand that agony forever. Something had to give.

Fortunately, I found a wonderful psychiatrist, Henry Leuchter, M.D., who guided me on my journey back to mental health. It took two years of weekly visits to him to work through my illness. I will be forever indebted to him for the work he did with me. He is an amazing man. I feel that he nourished my sense of authenticity and helped me become the person I am today. He is the most authentic man I have ever met. A true leader.

I must add that I do not feel I am completely "fixed". I believe that I am now, and forever will be in the process of healing myself. The issues that I brought to Dr. Leuchter are still with me, at times controlling me. I will never be completely free of them. My struggle to become whole is the driving force in my life, yet I understand that I will never completely succeed. My struggle to embrace the truth of my own limitations is a part of my own journey to authenticity.

It is very interesting to me that the concepts Dr. Leuchter taught me while working to extricate me from the clutches of mental illness have so much applicability in the field of leadership. In my experience in management, in my marriage, in raising a family, in getting my advanced degrees in business and psychology, in working with other leaders, and in much of the reading I have done, I can see the parallels of what he taught me to the field of leadership.

I have also had the opportunity to enhance Dr. Leuchter's teachings because I have had many wonderful mentors. In this book, I have attempted to point out the most salient parts of what I have learned about leadership and living a good life.

As you might guess, Louis, the main character in this book is me. Henry, my mentor, is an amalgamation of all of the mentors I have had in my life who have taught me so much about the subject of leadership and happiness. I also want to say that I do not perceive that I am writing this book from some tower of wisdom. I am in a daily struggle to become more authentically myself, often failing. I am deeply humbled by what I do not yet understand about leadership. I simply share what I have learned thus far on my quest for understanding. I hope it is helpful. I also hope that you will find it useful and immediately applicable in your life as a leader and your growth as a person.

I want to add a word of caution. This book is not a cure-all. I can remember when I was really sick I read many self-help books looking for the one answer that would cure my depression and end my agony. After I would apply what I had learned in those books I would feel even more inadequate because I was still depressed. If you are really stuck, don't be afraid to get some professional help. It will be the best investment you have ever made. In fact, I consider my mental illness the best thing that has ever happened to me, because it helped me see clearly that winning my self-respect was all that mattered in life. Those of you who scoff at these remarks, be careful. Mental illness affects millions of Americans. If you are not one of them, count yourself lucky.

I have had the privilege of helping many people in my career as a psychologist. I am now convinced that everyone has faced, is facing, or will face incredible amounts of pain in their lives. I believe that a person's ability to courageously navigate these trials will have much to do with their future as leaders and their happiness as individuals.

I want to make a final statement about the importance of leadership. While my main emphasis in writing this book was to help individuals on their paths to become better leaders, I feel a need to mention how important it is for all of us to reach inside of ourselves to find the leader within. We are living in a world beset by almost unimaginable problems: war, terrorism, disease, crime, poverty, etc. The list is endless. Sometimes it seems to me that these problems can never be solved because they appear to be so overwhelming. But I dream of a world where our children can grow up in peace and live lives of prosperity and happiness as they are meant to. I believe that human beings can live in harmony together in a world of tolerance, diversity, and respect. I believe this vision is within our grasp, if enough of us are willing to answer the call to authenticity.

Steve Anderson
Columbus, Ohio, 2003

Advance praise for *The Call to Authenticity:*

The Call to Authenticity by Steven Anderson has a wonderful energy. Today, more than ever, we need authentic people and leaders. Become one."

> Kenneth Blanchard, co-author *The One Minute Manager* And *The On-time, On-Target Manager*

"Steve Anderson has done extensive research on leaders and leadership. His book will help you learn what makes a good leader tick."

> Robert L. Bailey, author of *Plain Talk About Leadership*

"*The Call to Authenticity* is a creative story about the lessons of life... recommended reading for anyone developing themselves or others for success."

> Michael J. Anderson, CEO of The Andersons, Inc.

"A compelling read about one man's journey from pain and suffering to purpose and self discovery. You'll meet yourself often in these pages and come away with a renewed sense of the value of living and leading on purpose."

> Paula Butterfield, PhD, PCC, Executive Coach, Butterfield & Laning, LLC

"This book was truly inspiring; well written, fun to read and easy to implement."

> Adam Minton, CLU, Best, Hoovler and McTeague Insurance Services

"This book is great! Within a few short pages, it gets at what every organizational leader needs to know and what people sorely need! From my own experience in working with MBA students, I am so very much aware of how business leaders need to be in touch with their emotions rather than seeing them as an impediment. Steve Anderson has really nailed it on that one! I think this book has a wonderful potential to be helpful to busy managers and executives. It is easy to read, human, personable, and right on target! Steve taken the right stuff from the world of psychology research and practice and put it in terms that everyone can grasp."

> David Wallace, Director Counseling Center,
> Florida Atlantic University

"I found this book very enjoyable to read, as well as applicable in my daily life. It is written in a style that is fun and educational. I would recommend this book to anyone interested in improving themselves."

> Rishanna Denman, Network Engineering Specialist,
> Nationwide Insurance

"*The Call to Authenticity* has proven to be a valuable tool for me as a quality control manager. I found it enjoyable to read and immediately applicable to my job."

> Chuck Anderson, Quality Control Manager,
> The Andersons, Inc.

"I am immensely grateful to Steve Anderson for writing his book, *The Call to Authenticity*. In his book, Steve reveals several incredible kernels of wisdom that have significantly improved my effectiveness as a leader, mentor, and learner. He has also awakened in me a awareness of the profound impact that heartfelt dialogue and story telling have in connecting authentically with the people. I recommend this book to anyone interested in becoming a more effective and authentic leader."

Jim Anderson, President & CEO,
Key-Connections, Inc.

Chapter One

"The truth shall set you free, but first it will make you miserable."

Author unknown

"Damn it, Lisa, just do what I say!" snapped Louis. "Why the hell do you always have to argue?"

Lisa looked at him with moistened eyes, her lip trembling. As a tear trickled down her cheek, she said to him, "What has happened to you Louis? I used to like to work for you. I used to feel that we were on the same team." As her pain turned to anger she snapped, "Now I feel like you are whipping me every day!" With that she turned and marched out of the room.

Ouch. That got to him. Although it hurt, Louis knew she was right. What was going on? Lisa was a wonderful assistant. She really cared about the business. She was conscientious and hard working, and yet, here he was berating her.

What had gone wrong? Louis was thirty years old. He had graduated with his MBA five years earlier. He had come into this business with fire in his belly. He was going to shake up the business world. Some day, he had thought, he would be someone to be reckoned with. Everything had started out so well. He had achieved immediate results upon his entry into the business field. Sure, he wasn't all that popular, especially among those who worked for him, but wasn't that the price of success? "You either have to be liked or be successful," he had told himself. But slowly he had lost his edge. His department's results began to slip last year. His boss had told him in no uncertain terms to reverse that trend, or else. As Louis has pressed increasingly hard to hit his productivity goals, he had become progressively more difficult to work with. Even his wife was now complaining about his irritability. To make matters worse, he was feeling burned out and frustrated. He even noticed that he was having difficulty getting out of bed in the morning because he dreaded going into the office. He felt incredibly stuck and lost. He laid his head down on his desk in frustration.

Jim Rhubes, a friend, popped his head into Louis' office. "Want to play racquetball after work, buddy?" he said, as he opened the door and entered the room. Upon hearing Jim's voice, Louis slowly raised his head from his desk. Jim could see the pained expression on his face. "Boy, you don't look good. Everything all right?"

"Not really," admitted Louis, in an unusual display of vulnerability.

"What's wrong?" asked Jim.

"I wish I knew," said Louis. "Seems like I'm stuck and I can't get unstuck. I thought I knew how to do my job, but now I wonder. It seems like the harder I try the worse things get. Even my wife is getting sick of me."

"Plus, you're ugly," joked Jim.

"Not in the mood," replied Louis, somewhat irritated.

"Sorry about that," said Jim. "Seriously, you've got one thing going for you."

"What's that?" asked Louis.

"This is the first time you haven't blamed someone else for these problems," said Jim, "Now you actually have a chance of fixing it. I've held off from giving input in the past, because you seemed reluctant to listen, but I'll offer some now if you are interested."

"I'm all ears," said Louis, as he shifted in his chair and gave Jim his full attention.

"Looks like it's time for the 'Henry Treatment'," offered Jim.

"The what?" asked Louis.

"Henry is probably the best manager we have," said Jim. "He works over in the plant on Denman Avenue. The people who work over there rave about him. If you go over and see him I'll bet he can help you get the knots out of your rope."

"I'll try anything at this point," said Louis, exasperated.

"I'll write down his phone number," said Jim leaning over the desk and writing on a piece of paper on Louis' desk. Then he straightened up and smiled at Louis and said, "Thus endeth the lesson. So, do you still want to be humiliated in racquetball after work?"

"Earth to Jim, aren't you forgetting I creamed you last time?" said Louis.

"I went easy on you because you are such a klutz," chuckled Jim.

"Get out of here, you big turkey!" said Louis. "I'll see you tonight. And thanks for the advice. I appreciate it," said Louis.

"You're welcome," said Jim, as he withdrew from Louis' office.

Louis looked at the phone number in his hand. He felt a twinge of apprehension. Did he really need someone else' help? He had such a tough time making himself vulnerable, especially to people he didn't know. He thought about it for a minute and decided to take the risk. He had to do something. Maybe this guy could help get him unstuck. He picked up the phone and dialed the number. Henry answered the phone and Louis explained to him his predicament. Henry was intrigued.

"Do you want to come over and talk about it?" asked Henry.

"Sure," said Louis. "When can we get started?"

"How about if you come to my office right now?" asked Henry.

"Are you sure you can fit me in?" asked Louis, surprised.

"Sure," answered Henry.

"Okay, then. Let's do it," said Louis, feeling nervous, but excited. "Let me check with my boss and I'll be right over."

Louis was already impressed. Why would someone who didn't even know him be so willing to help? There was something different about this man. There was a calm confidence in his voice that Louis had seldom encountered.

Louis hurried down the hall and poked his head into his boss' office. "Molly, do you have a minute?" asked Louis.

"Sure," said Molly. "What's up?"

"As you know, I've felt frustrated for quite some time. Jim just stopped by and suggested I go talk to someone named Henry at our Denman Road plant. He said he thought he could help me out. I was wondering if I could head over there right now," said Louis, somewhat sheepishly.

"Do you have your sales reports done for the week?" asked Molly.

"Yes," said Louis.

"Well…you probably don't deserve it. You've been a pain in the neck lately!" said Molly, chuckling. "Awe, go ahead. I probably should have suggested the same thing a long time ago. He's a great guy. I think it will do you a lot of good to talk to him," she said, smiling. "Now get out of here before I change my mind."

"Thanks, boss! I really appreciate it!" replied Louis as he slipped out of her office and headed out to the parking lot.

As Louis drove over to the plant his excitement grew. Even though he was also feeling nervous, he had a sense something good was about to happen. Very soon he would realize what an understatement this was.

Louis walked into the front office of the plant and asked to see Henry. "He's out in the plant," said his secretary, Julie. "Just go out. He's waiting for you."

As Louis walked out into the plant he felt like a fool. "What am I doing here? I don't need anyone's help. This guy is going to think I am a failure," he thought to himself. He felt

23

so vulnerable approaching this man for help. He wanted to run and hide. Fortunately, Louis did not listen to his misgivings that day.

As Louis approached Henry he could see he was with one of his subordinates. Louis noticed that the employee was doing most of the talking. He could see the concern on Henry's face as he listened. Henry seemed to really care about what she was saying. Even though there was much activity going on all around him this man appeared to be perfectly at peace. Perfectly centered. At the end of their conversation, Louis heard Henry say, "Shelley, I feel that your judgment on this issue is right-on. Why don't you go with the supplier you suggested. If problems develop, let me know."

"Thanks for your feedback, boss. I'll let you know how it turns out," said Shelley. With that she smiled and turned away.

Louis was impressed with the confidence Henry was showing in his employee. Then Henry turned and looked at Louis.

"Hi, I'm Louis," he said, timidly.

Henry broke into a big smile and firmly shook Louis' hand. "Pleasure to meet you. I'm really glad you are here," he said.

"Are you sure you have time to see me now? Aren't you needed here in the plant?" said Louis.

"Oh, they can run this place without me," replied Henry, smiling. "I'm just here to sign the paychecks. They are the most motivated work force I have ever seen. I am a lucky man to have such talented people working with me. Let's go into my office where we won't be interrupted."

"Sounds good to me," replied Louis as he followed Henry into his office.

"Would you like a cup of coffee?" Henry asked, as Louis settled into a comfortable chair.

"That would be great," said Louis.

Henry poured two mugs of the steaming beverage, and handed one to Louis. Then he asked, "So what brings you all the way from the Zucker Road Plant to seek my assistance?"

"Well, for starters,' offered Louis, "I'd like to respond to what you just said about your employees."

"What was that?" inquired Henry.

"You said they were the most motivated work force you had ever seen," said Louis. "I wish I could say that about my employees. They are all lazy and untrustworthy."

"Well," said Henry, trying to think of a gentle way to say something that would be uncomfortable for Louis to hear, "that might have more to do with you than it has to do with them."

"What do you mean?" asked Louis.

"Let me answer your question with a story," replied Henry. "There once was a hardware salesman who had sued a local dairy farmer for selling him a supposed pound of butter that, in fact, only weighed fifteen ounces. As evidence in the trial, the salesman placed the butter, still in it's package on a scale in front of the judge. Sure enough, it weighed only fifteen ounces. 'He's a thief!' exclaimed the salesman, 'and I want justice!'

'Well, what about this?' the judge asked the farmer.

'Well, I don't own a scale,' admitted the farmer.

'You don't own a scale?' the judge asked incredulously. How can you sell butter by the pound if you don't own a scale?'

'Well, I do have a balance scale, just not one that shows weights on it. So, I decided to go and buy something I knew weighed a pound and use it as the counterbalance on my scale,' offered the farmer.

'What did you use for the counterweight?' inquired the judge, increasingly curious.

'A pound of nails I bought from the hardware salesman!" laughed the farmer, pointing at his accuser.

Louis guffawed. "Okay, okay, I get it," he said, as he shifted uncomfortably in his chair. " I suppose you are right about me, but I still don't get it. My employees won't do what I tell them to do. I was a top student in my MBA program. I feel like I really understand how to make a business successful, but no one wants to listen to me. I keep telling them what the goals of the department are, but it's like I'm talking to a wall. People today just don't care about striving for excellence. I swear, I was taught to always give my best effort, but it seems like others don't share this belief. I just don't get it! I will go over our priorities in a meeting, and as soon as I turn my back they ignore my direction and do whatever they want to. If I weren't there none of them would do a lick of work. It infuriates me!"

"Let me ask you a question," said Henry. "Why are you a manager?"

What a strange question, thought Louis, but he answered anyway. "Well...I guess because I want to be successful like my father was. I always looked up to him when I was growing up. I want him to be proud of me. I want to be a success!"

"But why management?" said Henry.

"It's the best arena in which to achieve financial success. My dad always taught me to be practical. I want to take good care of my family," replied Louis.

"Speaking of family, how's that going?" asked Henry.

"Not so well," replied Louis. " I love my wife, but she just doesn't get it. She's always telling me not to put in long hours. She wants to see more of me. But how am I going to succeed and take care of her if I don't dedicate myself to the job?"

"You know it's funny," said Henry, "The story you are telling me sounds like a very frustrating one. If I were you I would feel lost, even frightened, yet you sit there like a poised, self-assured person. Why?"

"I don't know what you are talking about," said Louis.

"What I'm saying is that I'll bet you are really hurting inside, but if someone was looking at us from outside my office they might assume you and I are talking about Sunday's ballgame. It's not obvious from looking at your body that you are struggling; yet your words tell me that you are. Your emotions don't appear to match the story you are telling me. I know this might make you uncomfortable, but you don't feel authentic to me."

"Well sure," said Louis. "I've always learned to be a poker player. Never let them see you sweat. Emotions just make you vulnerable and cloud the issues anyway. It's better to just ignore them."

"Is that right?" said Henry. "You think you'd be better off without your emotions?"

"Yes!" said Louis. "If I didn't get all emotional when I had to make decisions then I could reason perfectly. Emotions just muck up the works!"

"Interesting perspective. Would you be willing to consider another viewpoint?" asked Henry.

"Well, it would be hard to change my mind, but go ahead and try," said Louis.

"Okay if I start with a story?" asked Henry.

"Sure," said Louis.

"Once upon a time," began Henry. "there was a US naval ship in the North Atlantic. As they were steaming forward they received the following radio message from Canadian authorities: 'Please divert your course fifteen degrees to the north to avert a collision.' The captain of the US Ship replied: "Please divert your course 15 degrees to the south to avoid a collision. The Canadians replied: 'We say again, please divert course 15 degrees to the north to avoid a collision!' Back came the reply form commander of the US ship: 'This is the Battleship USS Missouri. We are a large warship of the US Navy. Divert your course now! After a moment of silence, back came the Canadian reply: 'This is a lighthouse… Your call.'"

"Great story," Louis laughed. "But, what's that got to do with emotions?"

"I just don't want you to end up on the rocks like that ship because you have made the wrong assumptions about emotions." answered Henry.

"Fair enough," said Louis. "I'll try to keep an open mind. Please explain to me why emotions are so important."

"Let's start with the most basic reason emotions exist. Why do you think we evolved to have emotions?" asked Henry.

"Why are you asking me this? And what the heck do emotions have to do with leading my team?" asked Louis.

"Bear with me," said Henry.

"Okay, that's easy, fight-flight. When our ancestors were threatened they had to get their emotions riled up to fight or run or they wouldn't have survived. They would become afraid; their hearts would start pumping, which would give them added strength and speed to elude their potential captors. But in case you haven't noticed, with the possible exception of my boss, there aren't too many predators roaming the hallways these days."

"So what?" said Henry.

"So emotions are outdated!" said Louis, defiantly. "They have outlived their usefulness. We'd all be a lot better off without them. You can't get all riled up when you are trying to make cool-headed business decisions," said Louis.

"Actually, you looked pretty riled up when you were describing the incompetence of your subordinates a little earlier," replied Henry, smiling slightly.

Damn, this guy was sharp, thought Louis. "That is so frustrating to me. As much as I hate getting emotional, I hate it even more when someone else notices it. It feels like I'm not in control of myself. I get so upset with myself when that happens. I think that I could be a good leader if I could learn to just completely suppress my emotions," Louis said.

"Sure of that, are you?" replied Henry.

"I think so," said Louis "Actually, I'm not sure of anything any more."

"See if this helps," suggested Henry. "There is a great deal of evidence that without emotions you would be completely ineffective, unable to hold a job, or be in any kind of a meaningful relationship (Damasio, 1994). Also, even though you think you'd be a good manager without your emotions, that is actually very unlikely (Goleman, 1995). When you ignore, or try to suppress, your emotions you are dismissing critical information you need to effectively deal with whatever situation you are facing. Also, possibly more importantly, if you were unable to feel empathy, it's likely that those who worked with would not feel you cared about them. People just don't seem to like to work for others who don't appear to care about them."

"That just doesn't make any sense," replied Louis. "When I become emotional I get all flustered or lose my temper and do things that are completely ineffective. You just can't be right." He felt more confused than ever. Perhaps he shouldn't have come, he thought to himself. Maybe Henry was a crackpot.

"You are right, getting too riled up is a problem, but so is being too 'chilled out' (Yerkes, Dodson, 1908). What you might consider, if you want to improve your performance, is to harness, not ignore, your emotions and learn to stay in your optimal arousal zone. Here, let me show you what this looks like on paper and he drew a graph on his dry erase board (see figure 1). Your optimal zone of arousal is an area where your

Figure 1

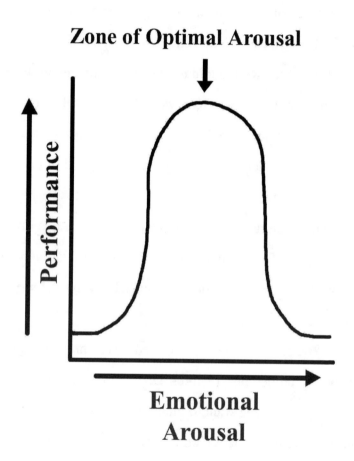

emotions are active, but not out of control," Henry said, pointing to the peak in the curve. "It appears to me, Louis, that you have been ignoring a critical part of yourself and it is impeding your effectiveness."

"That is scary," said Louis. "Emotions can be such uncomfortable, confusing things. How do you know what they are telling you? I've always avoided them because they didn't make any sense to me. Are you sure about this? Why can't I just solve my problems intellectually?"

"Actually, to be most effective you should combine your thoughts and emotions," answered Henry. "What I'm talking about is called emotional intelligence. An emotion is simply your body's physical response to whatever you are thinking about. For instance, when you become afraid you release adrenaline into your blood stream which causes your heart rate and blood pressure to increase. It's not so much what is going on in your environment that matters, but your beliefs about those events (Ellis, 1998).

"I'm still confused," admitted Louis.

"It can be confusing," comforted Henry. "Here let me draw it for you." Again he went to his dry erase board and drew the following diagram (see figure 2). "This is called the ABC's of emotional intelligence. First, something happens in your environment that activates the process (A). This information then passes through your belief system (B) as if it were a filter, or lens. This filter then directly affects your emotions (C). It is critical to understand that if your belief system is flawed, your emotions will not be appropriate for the situation, and can cause you significant problems. Also, if your emotional response is inappropriate, your behavior probably will be, as well."

"Can you give me an example?" asked Louis.

"Let me think," said Henry, pausing for a moment. "Okay, I have a good one. Let's say you and I were walking through the woods and we saw a Common Garter Snake. Now, if your belief is that all snakes are deadly, you might run away from a perfectly harmless situation."

"Makes sense," said Louis. "But how does that apply to work?"

"If, for instance," answered Henry, "your belief is that employees should do whatever their boss tells them without question, you will become visibly irritated when they challenge

36

Figure 2

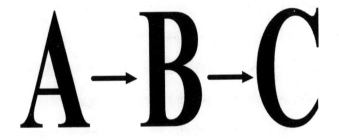

your directions, even if you don't mean to. Pretty soon, they will stop coming to you with concerns because they know what kind of reaction they will get."

"So, I can't hide my feelings from others?" asked Louis.

"Generally not, your body will express your emotions in some form," said Henry. "As you know, much communication is nonverbal. If you are angry there may be a change in the pitch of your voice. Your teeth might clench. Your eyes may narrow."

"Okay, I'm starting to get it, but please explain to me why this causes problems," said Louis.

"Because of the discrepancy between your emotional reaction and your self-perception, your behavior feels inauthentic to those around you, even if you don't intend it to," continued Henry. "What's worse is that you have developed a communication problem that is impossible to correct. Even if your employees did confront you about this discrepancy you probably wouldn't admit it because you are unaware of what you are feeling."

"You sound like you have a lot of experience with this, would you mind giving me an example from your life?" asked Louis.

Henry thought for a moment. "Yes," he began, "For years now I have struggled with a tendency to lecture people. Many people have pointed it out to me. I have thought about it many times, but I really only started to overcome this tendency when I realized I lectured others when I felt anxious in their presence. I realized that what they were saying was making me uncomfortable, so I went on and on instead of letting them argue with me. Once I realized how my emotions were getting the best of me, I have been able to steadily improve the situation. In fact, it has become a game. I invite others to tell me when I am lecturing them. This makes them feel more connected to me, and it gives me additional feedback to correct the problems. So now, what once was a problem has become a source of healing in my relationships."

"Wow, that really hit home. In fact, my wife sometimes says I seem angry, but I usually deny it," responded Louis. "Usually, after I cool down I realize she was right. It would be so much more helpful to realize what I am feeling when I am feeling it. So, apparently, I've been trying to suppress the very information I need to solve my problems, right?"

"And apparently succeeding," replied Henry.

"Why would I do that?" said Louis.

"Perhaps because feelings, at least negative ones, are painful to process," replied Henry. "People naturally avoid pain. Facing your negative emotions takes courage. In fact, in my opinion, that is what separates leaders from followers; the ability to adaptively address uncomfortable situations. Leaders are comfortable with discomfort."

"I still don't understand why I can't just figure all of this out intellectually," said Louis.

"That can't be answered for certain, but it appears that emotions focus the information in our brains into one feeling that we can use to solve problems (Damasio, 1994)," said Henry.

"Okay, I'll bite," he said. "So let's say I accept that I should pay attention to my emotions. How do I figure out what they mean? And what does all of this have to do with authenticity?" said Louis.

"Great question," replied Henry, "I believe that most people never make that inquiry. They remain blissfully unaware all of their lives that they are reacting to their emotions and the underlying belief systems that drive them. When we are able to truly understand our emotions and the beliefs that cause them, we can make them work for us. When we harness our emotions in this fashion, they become an incredibly powerful resource in helping us reach our potential as leaders. We harness our emotions by examining and destroying dysfunctional belief systems and replacing them with functional ones. Slowly, over time, our belief systems become increasingly adaptive."

"So, is emotional intelligence a quality of authentic leaders?" asked Louis.

"It appears that way," replied Henry. "I believe you will find that authentic leaders are able to connect emotionally to those whom they lead because they are so comfortable with their own emotions. They rarely feel threatened because they know they can productively navigate any emotions they have to deal with."

"Okay, I think I get it, but I still don't understand how I can become better at dealing with my emotions," said Louis. "How do I put the ABC's to work for me?"

"There are four steps you should follow," replied Henry. "I call them the four A's (Leuchter, 1984). You have to *acknowledge* what you are feeling. You have to *accept* what you are feeling. You have to *assess* what you are feeling. And you have to *act* upon your assessment."

"But what if it's the wrong action?" said Louis.

"So what?" replied Henry.

"I hate to make mistakes! They make me feel like a failure," said Louis.

"Mistakes are critical to the learning process. All authentic leaders allow themselves to make mistakes. In fact, the way I see it, people who don't make mistakes work for people who do."

"Are you sure?" asked Louis.

"I'm fairly convinced of it. Did you know that Thomas Edison failed ten thousand times in his attempts to create a workable light bulb? When someone asked him how he could persist after so many failures he replied, 'I didn't fail ten thousand times, I successfully found ten thousand ways that didn't work!' He also said, 'I had to succeed. I ran out of ways to do it wrong.'"

"Okay, perhaps I could become comfortable with making mistakes. But what is valuable about them?" asked Louis.

"The most important thing about making mistakes is that we can learn from them so that we do not repeat them. In short, if your action is maladaptive, go back to the beginning and acknowledge you made a mistake, accept it, then make a new assessment based on this information you now possess. Without emotional intelligence you might continue to react to your environment in the same dysfunctional manner forever. I feel that a common trait of all authentic leaders is that they have an unusual ability to tolerate and learn from mistakes. To do this, they have learned to sit with pain and not panic. Where others turn and run, they stay and face the pain and continue to learn from it."

"Can you give me an example of a leader who did this?" asked Louis.

"The best one I can think of is an account by Richard Byrd in his book *Alone* (1938). About eighty years ago, he spent the winter alone near the South Pole. On at least three occasions he was nearly killed, but by maintaining his poise he was able to successfully work his way through the problem that was threatening his existence."

"For instance?" asked Louis.

"At one point he was working outside and the door to his shelter froze shut," continued Henry. "Although he tried with all of his might he could not budge the door. He was locked outside in bitterly cold weather and heavy winds. He knew that he was doomed if he could not quickly get back inside. Everything inside of him wanted to panic, but he didn't. After coming to grips with the fact that he might die, he tried to think of a way to pry the door open. Once he was calm enough, he remembered that he had left a shovel outside a few days before. He dug around in the snow, found it, and pried the door open. If he had given in to panic, he most likely would have died."

"Okay, I think I am starting to appreciate the value of emotions, but how do I learn to understand what they mean, and use it to my benefit?" asked Louis. "It all feels like such a jumble of information to me."

"The most important thing I can tell you is to make time in your day, every day, to listen to what they are telling you," said Henry. "To do this you must be quiet. You can only hear what your emotions have to say when you are still. Then, I suggest that you write what you hear and make your plan based on this. In my experience, if you do not pay attention to your emotions, you will be their slave. If you harness them you will become master, not only of your emotions, but of your life."

"I sense you are right about the need to be still, but I'm still so confused. There is so much I still don't understand," said Louis.

"Sorry, Louis, but that's all the time I have today," said Henry. "I've got to get going. Can we meet at the same time next week?"

"Well, I hate to leave, but okay," said Louis as he stood to shake Henry's outstretched hand. As he left Henry's office he couldn't believe what he had learned from him already. Not wanting to forget anything, he wrote down some notes.

Summary: Meeting One

1) Emotions are caused by our belief
    systems, not from our environment.
    Functional beliefs cause functional
    emotional reactions. Dysfunctional
    beliefs cause dysfunctional emotional
    reactions.

2) If I understand my emotions I can
    restructure my underlying belief systems
    to enable me to actualize my potential as
    a leader.

3)   The way to develop emotional intelligence, is to take time every day to do the following checklist (the 4 A's):

Acknowledge what I am feeling.

Accept it! This is a critical step. If I don't accept what I feel I can never respond adaptively to it.

Assess what my emotions are telling me and make a plan of action based upon that assessment.

Act upon my plan.

Chapter Two

"If you want to (be a leader) in any kind of long term, committed way, you will need a vision that is truly your own- one that is deep and tenacious and that lies close to the core of who you believe yourself to be, what you value in your life, and where you see yourself going. Only the strength of such a dynamic vision and the motivation from which it springs can possibly keep you on this path year in and year out."

Jon Kabat-Zinn

The next week Louis arrived at Henry's door ten minutes early and eager to begin. "Can we get started?" said Louis.

"Sure," said Henry, looking up from his work. "Where would you like to begin?"

"When I left last week I felt like you still had so much to explain to me. I wonder if you have anything else you'd like to discuss," said Louis.

"Well, I have two questions to ask you, if that is okay," said Henry.

"Sure," said Louis.

"As I recall, you told me that your employees are not comfortable giving you feedback. Is that correct?" asked Henry.

"Yes, I would say that is true," admitted Louis.

"Do you see this as a problem?" asked Henry.

"Yes, but I don't think there is anything I can do about it. Like I said, no matter what I say, they won't give me input," offered Louis.

"As I suggested last week, that may be because you haven't been ready to listen. Perhaps because you were so certain that others were the source of your problems, they were not interested in helping," said Henry.

Louis remembered how Jim had told him that he hadn't wanted to tell Louis about Henry earlier because he hadn't seemed ready to listen. "I suppose you are right," admitted Louis.

"What do you think has kept you from welcoming input up to this point?" asked Henry.

"I never thought about it, but I suppose I was afraid of what I might hear if I listened," said Louis, hesitantly.

"See what happens when you are unaware of your emotions?" Henry pointed out.

"What do you mean?" asked Louis.

"Because you were unaware that you were afraid, you subconsciously behaved in ways that created safety for you by showing those around you that you didn't want their input. By admitting that you are afraid, you can show courage and seek the input even though it hurts," suggested Henry.

"I think I see what you are saying," said Louis. "Do people avoid what they are afraid of often?"

"Yes, in fact, I feel that most harmful behavior is driven by the avoidance of fear," answered Henry.

"I never realized that I was avoiding my fears before," said Louis. " How do I become more aware of them so that I can overcome them?"

"By regularly taking time to examine yourself and going through the four A's we talked about last week," said Henry.

"You're right, I don't do enough of that," admitted Louis, " but I'd like to start. The trouble is, I'm so busy I don't know where I could fit it in."

"Let me ask you a question," said Henry. "If you were taking a trip by car, would you make time to get gas, eat, sleep, and check your map?"

"Of course," answered Louis.

"Well, to continue with our travel analogy, it is just as critical to rest along life's journey to nourish ourselves and make sure we are headed in the right direction. You admit to feeling stuck, but you have no time to assess what is wrong with your situation. That could be because you see quiet time as a luxury. Once you start to realize that it is a critical part of a successful journey, you will build time for it into your schedule."

"Makes sense," admitted Louis. "If you don't mind, how do you do it?"

"Three ways," began Henry. "Every night I take a hot bath before I go to bed. I lie still and listen to my feelings. Once a week, I go to a local waterfall and sit still for ninety minutes. And once per year, I go on a retreat, by myself, and just listen."

"You're right," said Louis. "I just have to decide to make this a priority."

"I hope that you do. I believe that will be the single biggest factor in your future success as a leader," said Henry.

"That is very helpful. Thank you. Did you say there was something else you wanted to say about last week's discussion?" asked Louis.

"Yes, if you don't mind, I was uncomfortable with something you said about becoming a success," said Henry.

"What's wrong with wanting to become a success?" asked Louis

"Nothing, by itself. Wanting to be a success is good and healthy. That's not the problem. It's the way you talked about it that made me wonder. It seems like there is no alternative for you," said Henry.

"There isn't," replied Louis " I refuse to fail. Accepting failure is for losers."

"How is that strategy working for you?" queried Henry

"Not so well," Louis sighed. "As much as I refuse to fail somehow it seems to catch up to me, at least lately."

"And what happens when you do fail?" asked Henry.

"I become very discouraged and frustrated. I feel like a loser because I didn't meet my standard for performance. Then I start beating myself up, and start wondering about my ability, or I blame someone else for what went wrong. The problem is, I don't see any way out of this thought pattern. If I allow myself to fail I feel like I am giving myself an excuse not to put forth my best effort. I mean, aren't high levels of frustration natural when I have set my goals high and given my best effort?" asked Louis.

"Yes, but not to the point where you engage in self-flagellation," said Henry

"How do I get around that?" inquired Louis.

"First, I wonder if you could answer a question for me," said Henry.

"Sure," replied Louis.

"Could you please define success for me?" asked Henry.

"That's easy, achieving a desired result," said Louis.

"And what is the desired result you want?" said Henry.

"I want a to be a high level manager in our company. I want to get noticed. I want enough money so that I don't have to worry about how I am going to pay my bills. I want a great marriage and happy, successful children. I'd also like to have a big house and a lot of acreage out in the country," said Louis. "If I had all of that, I'd know I was a success."

"Sounds like a trap to me," said Henry.

"Why?" said Louis.

"You have so many expectations heaped up on yourself that the pressure must be immense," replied Henry.

"Not that I'm aware of," said Louis.

"Let me guess, every time you feel you are on track to make these goals a reality you feel good about yourself. Every time you come up short you get incredibly frustrated and beat yourself up. There is no in between. You're either on top of the world or you feel worthless," suggested Henry.

"Well…I guess so," admitted Louis.

"And how much of the time are you frustrated?" asked Henry.

"Most of the time, lately," acknowledged Louis.

"And whom do you usually blame?" asked Henry.

"Whoever screwed up my plans!" exclaimed Louis, unaware that he was raising his voice.

"Does that improve the situation or make it worse?" asked Henry.

"I never really thought about it, but I guess it makes it worse," said Louis.

"It also makes it impossible for you to change. You see, without realizing it you have made yourself powerless," said Henry. "You have to accept responsibility for your failures, or at least your part in them, if you hope to be able to learn from them."

"I guess that makes sense," conceded Louis.

"What if I could give you a definition of success where you could never fail?" asked Henry.

"Is that possible?" asked Louis.

"Sure, but you have to be willing to get your ego out of the driver's seat," said Henry. "You may not realize it, but you have let your need to be recognized by others gain control of your life. If you want to really be happy you have to change the way you think about success. You can't really control whether or not you achieve the results you mentioned earlier can you?"

"That sounds like a cop out to me," answered Louis. "If I give myself permission to fail, I can just stop trying. Sounds like a recipe for mediocrity to me."

"It can seem that way," acknowledged Henry. "But it's not. It's important to set goals. You need benchmarks to chart your progress. The difference is, you never stake your self worth on your results. If you shoot for the stars and hit the moon you still are in a pretty special place. It's in striving to be great that you achieve success, not in the goal attainment itself."

"Tough for me to accept, but I'll admit it is worth trying," said Louis. "So if I can't control my results, what can I control?"

"The way I see it, in life there are only two things you can control, the direction you choose and the effort you put into your chosen direction," said Henry. "Also, as I suggested last week. That direction has to come from within you. It has to be deeply and uniquely you."

"So what does direction have to do with success?" asked Louis.

"The really difficult thing to do in life is to learn to listen to your emotions, actually a better word for it in this case would be your soul, and to do its bidding with all of your might," said Henry. "I believe that every day our soul challenges us to live authentically, to follow our dreams, to be courageous. I believe that success is as simple as listening to this call, and then throwing ourselves into the journey our soul dictates to us."

"This still seems too ethereal to me," said Louis. "Can you explain it any other way?"

"Sure," said Henry. "The philosophy I am describing to you has an input oriented focus; not a results oriented focus. When you work to actualize your soul's vision you have already succeeded. You don't need some exterior reward to show you that you are a success. You already know it. You move with the quiet confidence of someone who has earned their own self-respect. Whether or not you get the results you wish for loses its importance. You become concerned with serving others and helping them on their way. The paradox here is that, normally, when you stop caring about external success you generally achieve it, because you relax and the solutions just seem to happen."

"Okay, that helps, but how do I get rid of my need for success?" asked Louis.

"You don't get rid of it, you just redefine it," replied Henry. "It's okay to say to yourself that you want external success. Your ego needs are important to recognize. You just have to know when to quit. You've got to be able to, at the end of the day, say to yourself, 'I did my best, and no matter what the results, I am proud of myself because I gave my best effort.' You have to *dare to be average*. That doesn't mean you put out average effort. You demand excellent effort from yourself, but you don't demand excellent results, because you can't control those. I want you to know, though, that this is never easy. I always struggle to keep this in focus. Like a little child, my ego screams to have its needs met. If I am disciplined and follow my heart that child gets exactly what it needs. If I give in directly to what the child wants, recognition, praise, the need to be liked, I always suffer and so do those around me. And I do make mistakes. It's inevitable. I am very charitable with myself when I do. I am human."

"So, I'm confused," said Louis. "If I focus only on my effort, how will I know when I have succeeded?"

"As I said earlier, it's okay to set goals," replied Henry. "You have to focus or you will probably fail. Can you imagine climbing Mount Everest without first setting a goal to make it to the top? What I am suggesting is that you don't have to achieve goals to feel good about yourself. Also, you will notice, as you become more authentic, that your goals have to do with serving others, not with enhancing your ego. It's hard to think of yourself as a loser when you are doing your best to help others. If you fall in love with the process of working toward the goals, then attainment of the goal becomes immaterial. As Ghandi said, 'Joy lies in the fight, in the attempt, in the suffering, not in the victory itself.' You are truly free. Your life suddenly becomes about serving others, not achieving some goal so you can feel good about yourself."

"Think about some of the great leaders that have existed; Ghandi, Lincoln, Mother Theresa, and Martin Luther King. These people achieved great fame, but that's not what motivated them. I believe that they lost themselves in the cause that their souls dictated. In doing so, they became great leaders."

"So in essence, leadership has nothing to do with who is following. It is obeying the marching orders of your soul as courageously as you are able. Is that correct?" asked Louis.

"Exactly!" exclaimed Henry.

"Wow, that really turns my whole philosophy of leadership on its ear!" said Louis. "When I look at leadership like this I can't get angry at others when I do not accomplish my goals. I am in control of my destiny and personal growth."

"Now you're getting it," said Henry.

"And the only way to fail is not to listen to my emotions or not to try," continued Louis "I am in complete control of my destiny. I determine what is important and I allow myself to decide whether or not I am a success."

"That's correct!" said Henry, smiling. "But, there is one last thing I'd like to suggest to you. If you really want to be a great leader, every day ask yourself if you are part of the solution or part of the problem. When you get committed to becoming a part of the solution you won't be able to stop leading."

"That makes a lot of sense. It's such an easy way to discern whether I am leading or following," said Louis.

"You're right," said Henry.

"Is there anything else for this week?" asked Louis, noting the time.

"Just one thing," said Henry. " One danger of this philosophy is that a person can become consumed by his/her passion. In order to achieve balance and happiness you must regularly assess your priorities so that all of the things that matter to you, like your family and friends, become a part of your vision."

"Good point," said Louis. "I guess I have been neglecting my family a bit lately. That's not fair to them. I guess I also need to work on my sense of balance as well. Thank you for your help."

"You're welcome," replied Henry, as he stood and grabbed his jacket. "Now I'd better get going. My wife told me that success this evening includes being home on time for dinner! Do you mind if we pick up from this point next week?"

"Of course not," replied Louis.

"Great, I'll see you then," replied Henry.

"Good bye," said Louis. With that, he grabbed his things and walked out to the parking lot. He realized what a gift Henry was in his life. The meetings he was having were completely changing his view of what was important in his life. Louis felt a growing respect for Henry. He realized that Henry was living his philosophy and it was making him an authentic leader. He could hardly wait to summarize his feelings. He pulled out his note pad and wrote:

Summary: Meeting Two

1)   When I work to actualize my soul's
vision, I have already succeeded.

2)   Results matter, but not as much as
focusing on my direction, efforts, and the
process of my journey.

3)   Leadership is not about who is following.
It is about being completely and
authentically myself every day.

4)   Every day ask myself, "Am I a part of the
solution or a part of the problem?"
Resolve to myself to become a part of the
solution.

5)   If I really want to be happy I must
constantly strive for balance.

Chapter Three

"Life is pain, Princess. Anyone who tells you anything different is selling something."

F. Morganstern, *The Princess Bride*

As Louis sat down for his third interview with Henry, he felt confused. He had so many questions. He felt that Henry had many of the answers he sought and he could hardly wait to begin.

"So what are your reactions to our meeting from last week?" asked Henry.

"Not what I expected," replied Louis.

"How so?" asked Henry

"Well, when I left here I was fired up," replied Louis.

"I have always felt like other people held control over my life. I unknowingly sought their approval. Last week, for the first time I saw how I could become master of my own destiny. After our meeting, I thought I could just get about the work of doing my soul's bidding. So, I set aside time on Saturday morning to be quiet, but I didn't like what I heard! I started to have dreams about what I could become, but I immediately became afraid. From that point on, I spent most of the week dealing with fear of all of the things that could go wrong on my journey to actualize myself. I was afraid everyone would laugh at me when they heard what I wanted to do. What is wrong with me?"

"Well, one thing's for certain," said Henry.

"What's that?" asked Louis.

"You paid attention last week," replied Henry. "Louis, the only way you know you are on your path is that there is no path. It's like you are chopping through the jungle. That process is inherently scary because you never know what is coming next."

"But I don't want to be uncomfortable. I don't want to be in pain," said Louis.

"Would you be better off if you did not feel pain?" asked Henry.

"Yes!" exclaimed Louis.

"Sure about that, are you?" said Henry.

"Sure, I would feel good all the time if I didn't feel pain, wouldn't I?" asked Louis, suddenly doubting himself.

"It's not likely," said Henry. "In fact, you'd probably be seriously injured, or dead in a fairly short time. Think about it; let's say you went home tonight and you walked into the kitchen to talk to your wife and you leaned up against a hot burner on the stove. You wouldn't know anything until your hand caught on fire. On the other hand, if you could feel pain you'd immediately withdraw your hand and barely injure yourself. Pain is there for a very good reason. It instructs you that there is something dangerous and you'd better be on the alert. You need pain to respond adaptively to your environment. Pain is a part of life. You'd better just get comfortable with that idea. In my experience, people who seek comfort at all costs inevitably end up becoming powerless and unhappy. Victims."

"So if we are always going to be in pain, what's the point of living?" asked Louis.

"Did you say you have children?" asked Henry.

"Yes, I have a one year-old daughter," said Louis.

"What is it like for you to hold her in your arms?" asked Henry.

"It's sublime; the most amazing experience I've ever had. I can't believe my wife and I created that incredible human being. She is a miracle!" said Louis.

"Then consider this; it is the same neurons that are sending pain signals to your brain also send you the signals of the warmth of your daughter's breath on your neck as you hold her in your arms. You can't have pleasure without pain," answered Henry.

"Isn't there any other way?" asked Louis. "I thought the idea of a life was to acquire enough wealth so that we could live in comfort and security for the rest of our lives, free of pain"

"Yuck!" said Henry. "How long do you think it would take for that to become boring. Do you know that Howard Hughes spent the last few years of his life sitting in a vault counting his money? Is that what you aspire to?"

"I never really thought about it. Perhaps it would become hollow," said Louis, looking somewhat confused. "But what's the point of life then?"

"The point is to give meaning to the pain," answered Henry.

"That doesn't make sense to me. Could you give me an example?" asked Louis.

"The best example I've ever heard of was in the book *Man's Search for Meaning* (1963). The author, Victor Fankl, was imprisoned in a Nazi death camp for several years. During that time, every member of his family was murdered in those camps. He nearly froze and starved to death many times. He and his comrades were forced to do hard labor every day. He watched as many of his comrades lost hope and died. He refused to give up, because he was determined to survive the war and help others learn from his own pain. Now, if that man can find meaning in pain of that intensity, you and I can surely do it at work."

"I don't understand. How do you give meaning to your pain?" asked Louis.

"Have you ever done anything that was very strenuous, but you really enjoyed it?" asked Henry.

"Sure, I backpack every summer. There are times when the pack straps are cutting into my shoulders and my whole body is exhausted, but I love it!" said Louis.

"Why do you love it?" asked Henry.

"There is nothing like being totally surrounded by nature. I never feel more alive than when I am standing by a mountain stream and watching the sun set in the middle of nowhere. I can feel the wind on my face, hear the water as it rushes past me, and smell the bed of pine needles beneath my feet. When I am out there, I feel an inner peace that I cannot articulate that penetrates me and makes me feel totally alive," said Louis.

"The reason you are enjoying yourself is because you are giving meaning to your pain," said Henry. "It's all worth it because you feel so alive. As a matter of fact, backpacking is an excellent analogy for a great life. Most of it is just plain dirty, sweaty work, but if you are doing something you love, then it can be wonderful. The analogy is also appropriate because there are two other things you must do to have a successful trip. You must take breaks to rest your body and you must fully immerse yourself in the experience. That is what is called enjoying the process of your journey. Getting to your endpoint is important. Enjoying the journey is everything."

"That is hard to believe!" said Louis "I never thought work could be as fulfilling as backpacking."

"Actually, I think it can be significantly more fulfilling for two reasons," said Henry. "The way you can really give meaning to your pain is to serve others. There is no better venue for this than your career. Your job is to figure out how to best serve by giving the gifts that are uniquely yours. When you realize that your gifts are sacred, you will no longer take the contribution you can make to this world lightly. Secondly, backpacking is something you can do for a week at a time. A career lasts a lifetime. In several decades of service you will have the opportunity to make an enormous impact upon others."

"But I get so afraid when I think about what my gifts are and what kind of an impact I might have on others. What if I fail?" asked Louis. "When I look at other leaders whom I respect, they seem so confident in themselves. I can't compare."

"I recall once hearing a story of a woman who was trapped in a sky scraper," replied Henry. "The floor underneath her was on fire. The leader of the group realized they were going to have to run down the stairs through the flames to survive. The woman who was telling the story panicked and screamed, 'We're all going to die!' At that point, another woman went up to her and grabbed her on both sides of her face. She looked into her eyes and shouted, 'Do it scared!' This calmed the woman down enough so that she and all of the others followed the leader to safety. Louis, anyone who has ever undertaken any project that requires all of their being has been afraid. Sometimes we just have to 'do it scared'. Try to imagine how Martin Luther King must have felt when confronted by hateful prejudice. He knew he was risking his life to live his dream, but it didn't stop him. The wonderful thing about fear is that when you face it and work through it, you transform yourself into a powerful vehicle to help others. You become an authentic leader."

"So leaders aren't self-confident?" asked Louis.

"They become self-confident," said Henry. "No one is really confident the first time they try something challenging, but once they face their fears and allow their passions to dictate their behaviors they become self-confident. Success is inevitable. Self confidence is nothing more than the belief that you can do whatever is necessary to achieve your objectives. Facing fears is how you achieve self-confidence. In fact, I believe that a hallmark of a leader is that he/she rarely panic when he/she is afraid."

"That's amazing," said Louis. "I always just assumed that confident people were never afraid."

"I don't think so," replied Henry. "The way I see it, courage is what defines a leader. Without fear there is no courage. Fear is the fire that galvanizes the will of leaders. Think about it, many who became great leaders, did so because of, not in spite of, extremely challenging circumstances. For Churchill it was World War Two, for Lincoln is was the Civil War, for Ghandi it was British oppression, and so on."

"So, it appears that I actually should welcome fear as a necessary part of the process of leading. Is that right?" asked Louis.

"Precisely," said Henry. "Your fear will help get you focused so that you can tackle obstacles enroute to your goal.

Learn to embrace, not avoid fear. Don't let it immobilize you. Realize that fear is an important component of success. It helps you become more focused and alert. Your fear will also show you the roadblocks to achieving your goals. I like to think of life as an oven. Fear is like the heat in that oven. It's as if you are made of clay. If you are courageous when you face the heat, you gain wisdom and you turn into something spectacular, like porcelain. If you run from the heat it will burn you up and you will turn to dust. Many teenagers today have stickers on their cars that say 'No Fear'. I say *know fear.*"

With this Henry turned and looked at the clock on his wall. "Well, young man," he said. "I've got to be going. Same time next week?"

"How could I say no?" answered Louis. " I can't tell you how much I appreciate your help." He shook Henry's hand and headed out to his car. "This is amazing," he thought to himself. The very thing he had dreaded for so long, fear, he now saw as a necessary ingredient for his success. For so long he had wondered if there was something wrong with him because he always became afraid when he dreamt of what he could become. Now he saw his fear as an ally in his quest to become a more authentic leader. Again, he sat down to write in his notebook.

Summary: Meeting Three

1) Fear is a gift and a necessary ingredient in the struggle to become an authentic leader.

2) Without fear there is no courage.

3) Fear helps get us focused and aroused in order that we may achieve our goals.

4) Pain is a part of life. The key to a great life is giving meaning to the pain.

5) What separates leaders from followers is how they deal with pain.

6) People who seek comfort at all costs end up making themselves powerless and miserable

Chapter Four

"Individual commitment to a group effort—that is what makes a team work, a company work, a society work, a civilization work."

Vince Lombardi

"What I've been thinking about all week", said Louis as he sat down in Henry's office, "is how do I get everyone on my team on the same page? How do I take everything you have taught me and turn it into teamwork? Do I just do the things you have suggested and wait for people to notice?"

"Actually, that would probably work, but there are many things you could do to speed the process along," said Henry. "Teambuilding is an art all its own. Even some great leaders are not necessarily great team builders."

"Can you give me some advice here? How do I go about this?" asked Louis.

"Remember when I talked to you about discovering your inner passion?" asked Henry.

"Yes," replied Louis.

"Your job is to develop the passions of your teammates into a collective vision, or mission. In fact, a shared sense of mission is one of the critical ingredients for success on any team (Reilly & Jones, 1974)."

"Makes sense to me, but how do I make that happen?" inquired Louis.

"You encourage them to discover and develop what excites them," Henry said. "Once they understand this, they will create their own vision of what the team can become, and how they can actualize their potential in that process. If an individual has a say in how a vision is created, they generally take ownership. It looks like this diagram (see figure 3; Senge, 1990). The way most teams operate is like the figure on the left. The outer arrow is the stated vision of the team. The inner arrows are the actual directions of the team members. Often the team members have not bought into the team's vision, or worse they don't even know what it is. There are few more frustrating experiences in life than being on a team that is fighting itself."

"You can say that again," offered Louis.

Figure 3

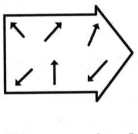

**Disorganized
Team**

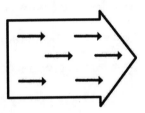

**Effective
Team**

"What is sad is that this appears to be the norm." offered Henry, "Do you know that most employees don't even understand what their companies are trying to achieve (Covey, 2003)? In Stephen Covey's words, 'Can you imagine if less than half of NASA's engineers understood that their agency's goal was to get to the moon?' "

"I'm getting lost here. What is the relevance of these figures to team building?" asked Louis.

"Well, the way I see it, a leader's goal is to have his/her team look like the figure on the right. In that picture all of the employees are working in the same direction and it is in keeping with the group's goals. There is alignment."

"That seems pretty simple on paper, but it hardly ever happens in reality, why?" asked Louis.

"I think that the problem," responded Henry, "is that many managers just expect their employees to know what they are trying to achieve without telling them clearly what that it is. Better yet, I think they ought to give them a say in setting the goals."

"Sounds good in theory, but how do I implement that concept" inquired Louis. "The way to do this is to build it into your weekly agenda. If you don't keep it on the front burner it will get replaced by seemingly more urgent matters that are begging to be addressed."

"Kind of like how you told me to make time to listen to my soul?" asked Louis.

"Exactly," said Henry. "Once you understand that getting input from your staff is a critical aspect of earning their commitment, you'll just naturally prioritize it. You can't expect people to buy into a mission unless they understand it and have a say in it. Also, some of the best ideas about how to move forward come from the employees. A good leader understands that his/her employees know more about what is going on at the front lines than they do. He/she allows them to have control of their small portion of the organization. To develop an effective team, the leader must understand that his/her job is to break down barriers in front of employees so that they can solve their own problems."

"Robert Greenleaf calls this concept *servant leadership* (2002). Unfortunately, it does not seem that most managers attempt to lead in this fashion. In fact, only ten percent of employees feel that their company fully empowers them to execute their goals (Covey, 2003). What I'm trying to tell you, Louis, is that you have a chance to do something special. If you really can harness what is unique about all of your employees they will love you for it and you will accomplish your organizational goals. The idea of empowering your team members is simple, but it takes tremendous effort and commitment to make it happen."

"I thought employees were motivated by things like pay increases and promotions," said Louis.

"That's what most managers think," said Henry. "In fact, I think that most managers are out of touch with what motivates their employees." Henry pulled a binder off his shelf and opened it. "Here's are the top three factors that managers think motivates employees in order of priority (Kovach, 1995)".

1) Good wages
2) Job security
3) Promotional opportunities

"That seems about right," said Louis.

"Now here's a list of what the employees said motivated them," continued Henry, opening the binder to another page.

1)   Interesting work
2)   Full appreciation for work done
3)   Feeling of being in on things

"As you can see, there is a considerable discrepancy between these two lists," said Henry. "Most managers would be much better team builders if they focused their efforts on what their employees say motivates them. I would also suggest that the best way to get the top three things on the employee's list is by harnessing the passion that we talked about earlier. Too many managers have ideas of motivation that came straight out of the 1950's.

"I have to be honest. I wonder if this will work. Every time I ask for input from my staff, I get little or no response," said Louis.

"It is possible, but difficult," offered Henry. "Your job is to create a trusting environment where people feel that their input is valued. This cannot be done overnight. The most critical change has to happen within you. You have to create space for your employees to step forward. There are always a brave few who will do this. When the others see you begin to implement the changes those few have suggested they will follow suit."

"What happens if the input I get is not consistent with the company guidelines?" asked Louis. "For instance, many employees have suggested that they be able to wear shorts on hot days, but it strictly against company policy. What do I do with those types of suggestions?" asked Louis.

"There are two issues here," said Henry. "First off all, no matter how ridiculous the suggestion, you have to take it seriously. If you dismiss the employee's concern out of hand they will be justifiably upset with you. Try to get to the underlying issue at hand. Perhaps the real problem you mentioned above is that employees wish it was cooler in the factory. Perhaps better ventilation, not shorts, is the answer to the problem. I think you will find that your employees will be motivated by your concern for their discomfort more than whether or not they actually get what they want."

"Second, you must recognize that there are some employees who do not belong with your organization. If it becomes evident that the direction they want to pursue is too disparate from your organization's goals, then you might assist them in their search to find an organization whose goals are more similar to their own."

"What about employees who just want to complain? Should I just let this happen? It seems destructive to my team," suggested Louis.

"Good point," said Henry. "Some employees are not interested in solutions, all they want to do is criticize, vent their frustrations, and blame others. This is poison to any organization and cannot be tolerated for long. Make it a policy that whenever anyone challenges what is being done that they have to offer a solution. Those that insist upon being negative must be removed from the organization or they will pull down the morale of the entire group. I once had the opportunity to ask John H. McConnell (2003), the founder of Worthington Industries, how he made his company so successful. He said,

'Treat people with trust and respect. If they show that they cannot be trusted, get them out, and quickly.' There are no simple answers here, Louis. What I want to impress upon you is that if you truly value input from your employees you'll get it. You just have to be patient."

"So what do I do when I get all of these suggestions?" asked Louis. "Won't I get overwhelmed trying to solve them? I'm already swamped."

"Who said you have to follow up on all of them?" replied Henry. "Get people on your team to follow up for you. The critical thing is to communicate. If you take the suggestions, but then never get back to your staff about what was done about it they will stop giving input and they will become cynical about this process. You will lose trust. I highly recommend you have a newsletter, bulletin board or regular meetings to communicate with your staff. Let them know clearly what is expected of them, what the organization's goals are, what their suggestions are and what is being done about them. I believe that communication is one of a leader's chief responsibilities. I can also assure you that once you get this process going your team will be unstoppable. Once you develop a sense of unity and mission on your team, the mood will completely change. It will be fun to come to work. When that happens, everyone wins."

"I must admit, this piece feels a bit overwhelming to me, but I want to try. I do care about my employees. I just have a hard time showing it," said Louis.

"Any risk you take in showing your true feelings of concern for your employees will be rewarded many times over by their happiness and improved performance," answered Henry. "The only thing that is stopping you from becoming completely authentic is your fear. Once again, if you courageously face that every day and fall in love with serving others you cannot help but succeed."

"I will do this!" pledged Louis. "I am eager to get started. I think I need to get busy applying the lessons you have taught me. Is it okay if we stop here?"

"Of course," said Henry.

"Can I call you if I get stuck?" asked Louis.

"You sure can," said Henry. "It has been a pleasure working with you. I hope it has been helpful."

"More than you can imagine. I can never thank you enough," said Louis.

"You're welcome," said Henry.

"Thanks, again!" said Louis, as he shook Henry's hand and left his office. As he walked out to his car, his mind was full of thought. He knew he would never again think of leadership the way he had before he had met Henry. For the first time in a long time he was excited about his chosen career path. But something seemed different. This time Louis knew he would succeed. In fact, he already had. He had made the decision to be the kind of authentic leader Henry had asked him to be. He realized that up until now, all too often he had been a part of the problem. He was determined, from this point on, to be a part of the solution. When he got to his car this is what he wrote.

Summary: Meeting Four

To create an effective team:

1) Create an environment where each person can actualize his/her potential.

2) Encourage authentic communication among team members about their passions and suggestions for improvement.

3) As a leader, courageously listen to the challenges your employees present.

4) Use the information from preceding steps to create a vision for the whole team.

5) Always follow up on your employee's suggestions.

6) Do your best to remove barriers to your employee's actualization.

7) Communicate, communicate, communicate.

After he was finished writing, Louis drove back to his office. He felt a renewed sense of purpose and direction. When he walked into the building his assistant, Lisa greeted him. Louis immediately felt guilty about how he had been treating this valuable employee. "Lisa, I appreciate the feedback you gave me a few weeks ago about my behavior,' he said. "I am very sorry about the way I have been treating you."

"Promise not to do it any more?" asked Lisa.

"Yes, I do," he said. " And I wonder if I could get your help with something."

Lisa had noticed subtle changes about her boss in the last several weeks. Gone was the irritability in his voice. He seemed calmer, more peaceful, more centered. She was actually enjoying working for him for a change. She wondered what had been going on in Louis' meetings with Henry over the last month. And now he was asking for her help. She could hardly believe her ears. "Sure," said Lisa. "How can I help?"

"Let's make this a place where everyone is thrilled to come to work. Let's make these employees feel like they are a treasured part of something really special," replied Louis.

"It would be a pleasure, Louis!" she said. And she followed him into the office. Louis was, indeed, on the road to authenticity.

Bibliography

Adler, Mortimer, J. Aristotle for Everybody. 1980, Bantam Books, Inc. NY, NY.

Byrd, Richard. Alone. 1938. G.P. Putnam and Sons, NY, NY.

Covey, Stephen, R. Information conveyed at a seminar entitled "Living leadership: The Power of Executing Greatness." 11/5/2003, Atlanta, GA. Information cited was from a Harris Poll of 11,045 respondents who were part of a U.S. active workforce from a variety of industries and professions. Results are accurate to within +/- 1%.

Damasio, Antonio, R. *Descartes Error: Emotion, Reason, and the Human Brain*, 1994, Grosset/Putnam, NY, NY.

Ellis, Albert, *How to Control of Your Anxiety Before it Controls You*. 1998, Citadel Press.

Frankl, Victor, E. Man's Search for Meaning. 1963. Simon & Schuster, NY, NY.

Greenleaf, Robert, K. *Servant Leadership: A Journey into the Nature of legitimate Power and Greatness.* 2002, Paulist Press, NY, NY.

Goleman, Daniel. *Emotional Intelligence: Why it Can Matter More Than IQ*, 1995, Bantam Books, NY, NY.

Kovach, Kenneth, A. "Employee Motivation: Addressing a Crucial Factor in Your Organization's Performance." Unpublished manuscript. 1995. George Mason University. Fairfax Virginia.

Leuchter, Henry. 1984, Personal discussions with the author.

McConnell, John, H. 2003. Personal discussion with the author. Columbus, Ohio.

Nachmanovitch, Stephen. *Free Play: The Power of Improvisation in Life and the Arts. 1990. Putnam Publishing, NY, NY.*

Reilly A. J. & Jones, J.E. *Team Building*. 1974. In J.W. Pfeiffer & J.E. Jones (Eds.), the 1974 *Annual Handbook for Group Facilitators*. San Diego, CA: University Associates.

Senge, Peter, M. The Fifth Discipline. The Art and Practice of the Learning Organization. 1990. Currency Doubleday. NY, NY.

Yerkes, Robert & Dodson, John. "The Relation of Strength of Stimulus to Rapidity of Habit Formation", 1908, Journal of Comparative Neurology and Psychology, 18, 459-482.

About the author:

Steve Anderson earned his undergraduate degree from The Ohio State University in Agricultural Business in 1980. He subsequently worked in several positions in the agriculture and retail industries. He achieved his Masters in Business Administration from Capital University in Columbus, Ohio in 1995. He attained his Ph.D. in Counseling Psychology from The Ohio State University in 1999. He is a licensed Psychologist. Since graduating, he has successfully developed his business, Integrated Leadership Systems, LLC. His focus in this business is to help organizations achieve their maximum potential by helping their members become more authentic leaders. He lives with his family in Columbus, Ohio. You can learn more about Steve at www.integratedleader.com. You can email him at steve@integratedleader.com.